RAPIDS

poems by

Daniel Wade

Finishing Line Press
Georgetown, Kentucky

RAPIDS

Publisher: Leah Huete de Maines
Editor: Christen Kincaid
Cover Art: Muno Bidhawat, of the Poolbeg Towers in Dublin
Author Photo: Graeme Coughlan: https://www.graemecphotography.com
Cover Design: Elizabeth Maines McCleavy

Order online: www.finishinglinepress.com
            also available on amazon.com

Author inquiries and mail orders:
Finishing Line Press
P. O. Box 1626
Georgetown, Kentucky 40324
U. S. A.

Table of Contents

City Limits

What Won't Happen Again 1
Side View 2
Escaping Silicon Docks.. 3
Draymen on Duke Street.. 4
Lion Country 5
In the Ivy Exchange... 6
Rapids.. 8
B.Y.O.G... 10
Pisshead Penance.. 12
From Private to Public 13
Red Cow Nocturne.. 15
In the National Stadium 16
Breadline Gladiators.. 17
Here, Paddy 18
Tattoos... 20
Frederick Street North, 11 September 2018...................................... 22
Prey... 23
Cumberland Street Dole Office 25
Shelter 26
Rooftop Blues... 27
Sea State Martello 28
Devil Eire... 30
Rope Jockey.. 35
Mountplesant Aubade... 37

Sea Batteries

Sea Batteries 41
Oar.. 42
Immram.. 43
Bádóirí 44
Rescue 116 46
The Signal Fire 47
Carrier.. 49

The Long Watch 50

Maude Jane Delap..51

John de Courcy Ireland..52

Sandeel Bay..54

Granuaile 55

Navigator 57

Achaemenides...58

Passage Plan 62

Breath 63

Bearings 65

The Liner *Reina del Pacifico* during Sea Trials...............................66

A Volunteer 70

Salvors' Reach...72

Borders

On the Shooting of Lyra McKee in Derry 75

As Leaves or Thieves 76

Violet Gibson 77

Spring in the Sablon 78

Monkey Gone to Heaven...79

Lion's Den 80

Border Crossing..82

Hush 83

Beltane Fire Festival in Edinburgh..84

Outage..85

After the Bailey 86

Provence, 2016 87

Cais du Colunas..88

Two Visionaries 89

Pebbles 91

The Blind Leading the Legless 92

Warmth 94

Blues for Louis 95

Acknowledgements 96

City Limits

What Won't Happen Again

Her reaching for my chin, to pull me in for a kiss, won't happen
again. Nor will the dawn chill, snapping us awake,

as her bare heel rubs coldly off mine under the blanket;
kisses that stand for ceremony, kisses preluding a headache

or sex. Also, walking each other to work in the morning, waiting
in line at Starbucks for nosh and caffeine, before break-

ing apart and make for our separate daily treadmills; the white
roses I'd buy her, the coffee I could never properly make.

Her refusal to observe any of her birthdays, wearing
my white hoodie to bed, or meeting up on her lunch break.

Her smiling, shut-eyed, as I aimed the blow dryer at her head,
her hair cannonading, whipped smooth and opaque

in a spray. I lack her skill for letting the past go easily, you see,
whether at home or in a supermarket aisle, so for the sake

of preserving the grace she left behind, above all else—I allow
none of this will happen again, whatever I return, steal, give, or take.

Side View

Not sure where I am, exactly: the wind's icy babble
around cast-iron rails, sputtering cross-city wires
above an unbuilt LUAS stop, a Brazilian rickshaw driver
checking his phone

before the night gets busy. Might I call him friend,
or follower? I double-tap a thousand profiles
before seeing yours; then, and only then, do I know
that love is unavoidable.

I try teaching myself your language, the warp
of its adjectives, the way the verbs squat on the tongue,
your glossary's proper pronunciation.
Do I now have your approval?

A single glitch is all it takes for the Leap Card
to deny me any kind of entry, any kind of leave;
crushed beer cans soak the fire exit,
skips from KeyWaste brim over

with black, bloated bags at the Green Line depot.
At last call, the Stag's Head becomes a submarine,
its radars tuned to a garbled frequency.
"Dublin's fair city? Ask me bollix…"

Bone-hard wrists folded tight, she tries sleeping
in a doorway, her shelter of damp cardboard
and piss-damp sleeping bag. Might I ask her
name, even? Across the street,

a Motorway Maintenance crew ebonises
the curb, slow cell growth seepage; I still haven't
a clue where I am. "What else are you, but a ghost?"
Diesel fumes, dizzying, curl to my gullet.

Escaping Silicon Docks

A snarl of traffic, backed up as far as Finglas,
could easily be Joe and Jill Bloggs fleeing the city
for safer ground. Sleek monoliths of glass
and steel loiter in their wake, the canal's eye
rolling under mod con and masterplan,
where blanch of mildew soils the cornucopia
of startups linked by shatterproof skybridge:
too many are sleeping rough in this utopia.
Look at that conference of seagulls nestle
under Alto Vetro, the sun crimson
as a shaving cut, and cranes loom afresh
above the quay's pewter ledge—
may civilization never declare itself civil.
But don't mind the hipsters who hog the plaza
headset-plugged and ogling their tablets,
typing, retyping botched Wi-Fi codes,
or the manhole clanking its gripe of rust
under your foot. There's more to this low-rise world
you claim as your own: whispered threats
kneading the air as rush-hour crowds pitch
and roll at traffic lights, dodging cracks
and cycle-lanes, bus convoys and LUAS
clangs, eagle-eyed bouncers vigilating
in doorways, neon glint from Supermac's
leaking out while haggard junkies lurch
between taxi rank and double-yellows,
homeless in their hometown, a girl
huddled in a sleeping bag under the GPO's
bullet-bejewelled portico, and a lone Garda
struts by her without salience.
As for me, I sweep and scrub the floor
of the canal, dredge up nameless stones
squeezed dry of blood, with my sunken chance
in this boom of dawn, sky, and traffic cones.

Draymen on Duke Street

They arrive with the dawn's crisp bite, and snore of traffic.
I hear them before I see them: stainless-steel clank
On cobblestone, each keg stamped with the year
It were made, mostly scuffed, and far older than me.

The lads've only a few seconds to unload from the lorry
To cellar before the next one rolls along.
A steel-cap boot snakes out, halts it on the curb; gloved hands

Upend it, flip it down the hatch's yawning maw.

They keep up this ballet of knee-lift and high-viz for twenty
Minutes or so before making a move. Always another
Delivery or docket to sign as they make for the surrounds,
Their eyes slowly hit by the sun's radiant puncture.

Lion Country

He stood next to Michael Collins' grave
wearing Raybans and a pinstripe suit
he wore only for funerals or court hearings,
and played 'Lark in the Clear Air'
on his tin whistle in unrehearsed tribute.

The crosses of Glasnevin Cemetery heard nothing,
saw nothing, carried the makings
of silence for long enough 'til the supreme trumpet
wrenched the dead back from repose.

But there were no trumpets for now,
just the tin whistle's melodic squeal,
the exhaled sorrow and slender notes
billowing their way skyward.

Once, he'd have bartered with tempters,
haggled over ghoulish prices and numbers
just for the privilege of stepping into Lion
Country:

the river of arpeggios soaking the air
to a bodhrán's thunk,
blood seeping from the fault line in every rock,
ghost dancers thrashing on open ground,

caves where daylight was outlawed,
flowers scorched, mountains burst
asunder by rainfall,
tears drying up as he kept uncertain time.

In the Ivy Exchange

For Karl Parkinson

'the rain falls that had not been falling and it is the same world...'
—George Oppen, *Of Being Numerous.*

Rain: my 95th favorite type of weather.
Doesn't take much to remind me, sure it doesn't,
now that I sing of all that I ever wasn't
with very little song left in me? However,

before starting work, I walk past the Ilac,
freestanding in certainty, the whir of a street-
sweeper sucking up cigarette butts
down Henry Place, where a dreadlock-

ed junkie, face color-bled, squats mid-shite
in a shuttered doorway, unmoved by the combined
reek of aerosol spray, weed and fish waft-
ing up from Moore Street on the wind

into morning traffic, where a Deliveroo cyclist
pedals through a red light, and Gardaí shuffle
by on patrol. I clock in, stand my daily post
at the Chapters Bookstore entrance, muffle

back yawns no Americano could quench,
eye each and every face that walks in,
waterproof Timberlands planted firm.
The automatic doors stay stubbornly open,

air-flows hiss across parquet tiles to knock over
the yellow 'Caution Wet FloorTM' folding sign
as rainy footprints pool their displeasure,
like barcodes stamped to clear.

Tannoy blares Vivaldi in the morning and Bach
at noon, the sweet, dread chorus

of *St. Matthew Passion* a call to prayer for waifs
and strays to amble in, spill vodka in the kid's

section; it doesn't drown out the mid-afternoon
swarm of Toyota, Citroen and Skoda chariots
trampling after eternity. In March, Parnell's crown
is bulldozed, ashtray-destitute, traffic lights

grinning a salutation at me with the green,
and give me the finger with the red.
"You're only makin' more work for yourself,"
the assistant manager grunts, shaking his head.

For sure, it's Dublin's answer to Times Square (circa '72),
and twice as much of a shithole; even the iron shriek
of the Broombridge-bound LUAS is bandaged
in frost. But it's only rain that falls, adding acidic

wealth to the pavement once the tide ebbs back
to ground-level. I clock out at half six, switch my phone on,
thumb through notifications, go for a gargle
in Fibbers. Later, I'll carry a shopping bag laden

with empties to the bottle-bank behind Tesco
and head home to you the scraps of rain,
when I'm done with their shattering, now
bone-weary, and soaked to the skin.

Rapids

When he got kicked out in second year for
smoking hash on the Astroturf, relief
heaved from everyone's throat. No longer
would we have to fear
his ape-like strut, fists' basalt salvo,
rain-grey tracksuit, knife-like stare.
There were lads two, three years older
scared shitless of him.

A box off him left you bruised, winded; your
gashed mouth inhaled gravel
as his Reeboks slapped off asphalt,
his knuckles flexed, re-flexed bone-white. He
reminded us that, next to him,
we were still only kids, mammy's boys softened
by affections he probably
never had, our innocence mortifying
and bared, our voices still reedy,
cracked against his surly baritone,

our reluctance to hit back, give him
a taste of his own savagery, secure. His fist
held the key to every hard-bitten door.
He shook it, a tattooed incitement to war,
spelling out the value of hatred in school.
Yes, his hatred had been welcome.
As welcome as it was mutual.

I heard he tried topping himself later.
Years of dejection boiled down to it before
he lobbed himself into the stream near
his estate, hoping to either bash his skull off
sunken rocks or else drown in the rapids
set his body afloat like fleshy driftwood.

After they pulled him out, he was at first
unresponsive to the C.P.R before

his eyes snapped open and a few choked
fuck you's bubbled and fizzed off
his tongue; when he was fully woke,
lava dribbled from his mouth.

B.Y.O.G.

Bring your own gargle, and don't act the prick.
Let your excitement fizz. A rakeload of cans,
Bavaria or Lech, from a nearby Lidl
(we go splitsies), the plastic bag torn flimsily open
before our crushed empties sink in a pile
to the canal's muddy floor. A swan
tucks its ivory wing, glides off for a paddle
with the breeze. An ephemeral spark
fizzes from the bench where we sit
'til one of the lads leaps in, to hollers of, "G'wan
y'mad thing," and "geebag", silently hoping
he won't resurface soaked in shit.

Our voices drown in the soothing rush
of water as it flushes under scarred
lock gates, tunes throbbing from
the pub up the way. Plenty of hash
and yokes to go 'round, and street fire,
wild street fire, is kindled, frothy scum
bubbling to the surface with our laughter,
grass and twigs set adrift. It's grand, it's enough
for the passing, sideways glance of a guard
to be averted, like a chewed-up gum.
Yeah, the buzz spreads like absolute wildfire.
Tonight, duty and solemnity can fuck off.

Cans by the canal. The sun in copper leeway.
All the summer ecstasy went for cheap,
so we're off getting gee-eyed on Good Friday
in the city that never sweeps.
Barges are moored glumly to sloping banks
where I lie, watching the ebb roil like diesel,
sharing a spliff with lads I haven't seen in yonks.
Would I get the same thrill if any of this was legal?
And swim or sink, the option to quit's

always there, the memory mine to sculpt:
even with the arse frozen off me, it's worth it

for the sting and haze, slumped on a dock under
Charlemont bridge, shaken by the LUAS' shunt,
shoulders arched against the cold. Cider
makes a furnace of my throat, as I hock and grunt
to where cigarettes scowl like low-tar beacons.
Off someone's phone, I hear a soft growl and chortle,
soundtrack to a city's life after dark.
I'm in flying form now, I can't complain;
I look forward to the walk home, where I'll
trip over wheelie bins and stumble into trees.
I look forward to the hangover, even,

because this is a real session, for real people.
Lashings of music mumble prayers on the baritone
wind as we quiet down—the chewed-up, gleeful
bolus of our banter spat out, as if from a cup.
All this, I choose to remember, forget or atone
for, the eventide rippling silver to my eye;
but home now beckons, and I'm sobering up.
So, like rabid dogs that stretch their leashes
we snarl the height of abuse at passer-by, 'til
the last can is downed, and the canal speechless.

Pisshead Penance

In the jacks,
on my knees before the bowl
as if repenting, bile
and blood-laced mucous
drips off my chin
and my chest, a self-hollowing pit.
I hear someone enter
and sidestep the piss puddles,
stand at the trough, unzip,
start pissing. If he can hear my hocked
retches, he ignores them.
After a while,
the hand dryer roars to life
and the door slams shut a little later,
and I can just about
make out the graffiti scratched
into the door again.
'BRITS OUT 26 + 6 = 1 32 county
"FREE EIRE"
or 'arrest the pope'
or 'lotto scam'
or 'HANNAH
regan
gives
Good
head'
... is what I think it says.

From Private to Public

I'd see him the odd time up in the Igo,
skulling a Bulmers as instant replays
of the Aston Villa—Arsenal game'd

play out on the overhead screen. He'd barrel
out of the jacks, thumb jerked
at the bar by way of offering a pint,

or else jangle his keys as if reminding
himself. They'd click and snap
together, blurred as a locust's wing

as he checked his phone by the cigarette machine,
had a smoke outside, I.D. card
on his belt, slagging off everyone in sight.

Always good craic, being in his company.
'Til you sat down with him, one-on-one. "Me?
Sure, I'm not worth gettin' to know," he'd say.

"'Course I'll head ou', have a gargle, play
a bitta pool or darts, be the quickest with a joke.
Why wouldn't I, sure? Laughter comes easy

to the likes of me. Tell me to sling me hook
and I will, no bother. Public affairs? Really
not my bag, know what I mean? Sure look,

biggest mistake I ever made was goin'
from private to fuckin' public. I know who
I am, and what I am. I'm just better off

at a safe distance, is all. Sure, me exes'll
all agree: I'm not worth gettin' to know,
not as a mate, and definitely not as fella

or a husband. Am I lonely? Fuckin' sure.

Wouldn't be human I wasn't. But I'm used
to it, y'know? Immune to it, y'might say.
Here, lemme tell yeh, biggest mistake

I ever made was goin' from private
to fuckin' public. Few laughs is all
I'm good for. After that, don't bother."

Red Cow Nocturne

The moon, half-cut like a pineapple slice and
sugared with stars, weighs in with just
the right angle, at just the right time;

gunmetal clouds drop payloads of mist and
drizzle over the carpark, wheezing wind coughs
up a crumpled chip bag for autumn.

You can stay where you are, the exit sign
glistening above you, purr of traffic
and whipped splash of a puddle overturned

by a tyre's swipe; as the cold bites down harder,
its swirling teeth leave you burned.
To leave this place, first you'll have to kick.

In the National Stadium

Encased in the four corners of the ring,
Before laying down face or name,
The boxers stand ready for the gong,
Middleweights on the brink of fame.
What are they without rivalry's impact?
Isn't blood a fact of the prize-fighting life?
The rough edges for keeping pride intact,
Branding irons to scald the other's life?
And do I share their hunger for success,
The impregnable resolve to be a title holder,
To floor an enemy after four rounds or less,
If I have no invidious scar to gloat over?
Better men than me have stood in that ring,
Battled and bruised, slumped on its canvas: Has-
beens, greenhorns, all the latent kings
Of the Stadium, facing failures they'll surpass.

Breadline Gladiators

I ran into him at the bar in Workman's.
I felt the old hatred bubbling like grease.
Still, I asked him how he was getting on.
Said he was good, yeah, studying overseas.
Was I still in college, working or signing on?
 In the smoking area, I said, "Ah, in-between
At the moment. Handing in C.V.s where I can.
Haven't found much yet." He looked obscene
As he replied, "Yer not lookin' hard enough."
Disdain thinned his smile. He said a mate got him
A cashier's job at KFC. My penury pleased him.
Shame made me fidget, like he'd called my bluff.
If I lost the head now, I'd only be admitting defeat.
He offered me a pint. To save face, I accepted it.

Here, Paddy

Here, Paddy, I work in one of the Baggot Street
pubs where you and Brendan Behan used to get rat-arsed
back in the bad old days. I'm inquiring for you nightly,
as per your song's instructions, but I've yet to hear
a good answer. They were sound enough to print
and frame some of your poems on the wall,
and not just the ones everyone knows, either.
I wonder if some of your best lines came to you here,
gutted and gargled and sunk on a barstool?
How much of your betting money was pissed away
in the snug, smoked hover of fog smearing
the window like halitosis, streetlamps kneaded
like well-oiled hearts? Did you grope for a few coins
clanking in your pocket, a final pint to dim the view?
Did you end up getting barred from here, too?

Here, Paddy, I work when everyone else parties.
When everyone else works, I sleep. Maybe
your ghost will shamble in here some night soon,
your pipe lit just in time for last orders, and we'll have
ourselves a final lock-in together. The place won't be
as you'd remember it, though. We serve vodka
and lime in cocktail glasses, and there's more craft beer
on tap and draught than stout—stuff I'll bet
you'd never have touched, even if you were on fire.
Or maybe you would have. Who's to say?
You might drink whatever I put in front of you while
I polish and re-polish down the bar
you probably shattered untold shot glasses over.

Here, Paddy, have one on me. I read you almost
drowned one night after walking home from here, in
the same canal that gave you your sonnets
and restored your faith. Did you ever spew your
cantankerous guts up in the alley out by the beer
garden, where I'll later on dump tonight's waste?
Were your raven-black lungs bleached white

by the water's cold swirl, pouring deathly and sore?
Such is the purge: glint of a cross, the surround-sound
PA spewing its woeful eighties playlist,
the age as golden as the calf you bled from its plinth of
piety. The evening's ash, swept from the ground,
is a heap of glass and God-knows-what shame.
What noble savagery starved you in this month
of fasting, when you'd vent your homily of flame?

Here, Paddy, I'll be honest with you: I haven't read
much of your poems in a while. I've forgotten
their magic. Supplicant of field, cartographer of cloud, your
passionate transitory can't be found here, no *Eden*
flowering in a poet's mind, as you might say,
can be spoken of or enjoyed on a smoke break.
The way your hills turned black, cattle trudging ahead
of a plough, a girl's dark hair woven like a snare
to enchant the cobbled way you forced yourself
to pass along, canal water warbling: all too far removed
from the emptied keg, the ever-changing roster,
the lounge heaving and black with bodies.

Here, Paddy, it's hard to get inspired when you're
mopping up vomit dregs or crushing wine bottles
at three in the morning, and all for the sake
of €9.25 an hour. Strain of ballads trapped
in your threadbare throat, another whiskey to pour
at the void, your eyes' glint watered down
to blindness: none of these kept you from the threshing floor's
density. As for me, fatigue bites my footstep,
swings and clamps its bulky leg over my shoulder.
The last punter's gone, the bar is stocked and ready
for tomorrow night's piss-up, beermats
are still crumpled and soggy with dew. It's then I worry
about going skint, bills unpaid, skull emptied, shirt rumpled.
But then, isn't this the lesson you left to us all, Paddy?
To glean poetry from the least poetic of moments?

Tattoos

i.m. Paul Curran

I saw you three times the week you
killed yourself. But I spoke to you
only the once.

First time, you came into where I work,
and we'd a brief catch-up, chatting about
where we were at since we last spoke,
our girlfriends, the burdens of language,
what gigs we both had lined up
(none for me, and a fair few for you).

Second time was in passing, and I didn't call
out or catch your eye in time.
Third time, smoking in the Dame Tavern
doorway with your mates, and again,
I said nothing; just kept on walking.

Each time, there wasn't a bother on you.

*

As proud Northsider and unsure Southsider
we'd cheerfully slag each other off,
our Liffey-edged polarities swirling in laughter
'til you'd say, "Northbound or south,
man, what's it really bleedin' matter?"

*

I can't say I knew you that well, Paul, but I did know
you were sound, a skin decent enough
to absorb indelible ink, no faded tattoos on show.

At EP, over campfire embers, you planted your Docs
in the grass and your rebel bearing flared

as you recited poems of Coolock, concrete site
of your youth, ageing backroads, MacGregor

and Lamar, John Keats and Joy Division, mates

lost to gunshots and *the art that never gets made*.

No-one guessed you were more fluent
in the grammar of eulogy than any of us.
So who knew it would settle on you,
the abrupt beckoning of death?

There isn't a lot to apologise for now, Paul.
I've only your Soundcloud left on repeat, now,
and your voice's pulse, keeping me on the ball.

Frederick Street North, 11 September 2018

On Frederick Street North, an unmarked van pulled away
Into rush-hour, as if to make way
For the traffic's slow air and baton stomp, pepper spray
Festering our faces. Names inked in blood that day

Were quickly crossed out, scribbled over, or pocked
With small scarlet X's, each stamped with a crude target
Sign. Fist and balaclava were the combination to keep us locked
Out, near the traffic light that showed itself as a derelict

Sun by the empty building with its front doors
Smashed off their hinge. Merely a matter of course,
The riot squad forming a blue-black chorus
Line, clamped with boots of clay:
Occupation peaceful as an angle grinder's buzz.

On Frederick Street North, site of our unwritten fray,
We march into chaos again, overworked
To each election pledge's glass hilt, without delay,
Braced for the city's scorn, and see it usurped.

Prey

My face scraped along
the span of concrete
when I hit the footpath,
brunt of a boot heel
pumping air from my chest
over and over, cut-
price reek of aftershave
or diesel over Cabra Road
their half-dead eyes

slashing me down to size,
feeding ravenously
on fist-spasm, on headbutt,
garbled roars echoing,
half-dead eyes glistening
in the fine, cool, neon,
smoke-free night. My own
vision a red-lidded mesh
of gravel and tar, the moon

bulging like their knuckles,
like the black eye I'd have by
morning. It was a while
before they stopped.
Arms sprawled weightless,
face a chewed-off pulp,
I felt the flavour of blood
ripple on my tongue, my teeth,

like a flint-eyed snake coiling up
to bite down hard on its own tail.
Wild dogs in hoods, drooling
shade and glee, skulk in unison,
fangs glinting in the laneway,
closer. Good thing I didn't
end up as a vegetable afterward.
What weakness of mine did

the bloodhounds sniff out?
I was too soft to fight back, I guess,
make it worse, and anyway,
what was my word against theirs? What prize did they want
off me, and to what end?
Truth of the matter is we need
to compete, to contend.

Raindrops fell to marinate
the blood. I staggered the rest
of the way home, orange
icicles glittering off tonight's
scrimmage. No charges pressed.
Ribs in bits, bones hollered
and howled, but I could
still breathe, a jerry-rig
of limbs shuffling to heel.

Cumberland Street Dole Office

Light glowers from a cheerless ceiling
where the arc lamps hover over the heads
of everyone in the queue, mutely crackling:
the jobless rank-and-file, the whites and reds
of our eyes bulge like soft jewels. No intercession,
no setting apart. Men in business suits stand next
to sacked plumbers. After ten years of recession,
we can still laugh stiffly at our annexed lives:
each face smeared with the invisible manna
of humiliation, each eye inflamed with the glaucoma
of fear, every neck breaking out in sheepish hives.
All of us here understand what little we're worth.
We don't see or hear anything in this idle nirvana,
except the frozen-over flames of our mirth.

Shelter

The story, as I understand it, goes like this:
at a certain point, in the early hours of dawn,
a man shuffles into the ED waiting room
of Tallaght Hospital, where, amid intercom trills,
broken limbs and bloodied tissue, he quietly
takes his place in the queue. He doesn't check
himself in, seek medical treatment, or receive triage.
He merely sits, a picture of passivity, hands on lap,
looking for all the world like he's asleep, dosed off
from the boredom of waiting; (later on, some
even joke it was boredom that finished him).
And here's where the story gets strange.
No one can say how long he's been there,
few hours to a day. They can't say when exactly
he checked out, or how. They pass him
in the corridor, lost in their own injuries
and complaints, busy with phones
or frayed magazines before the blue-faced corpse
is finally noticed. The very thing they all no doubt
dread hearing from a doctor's lips is seated
slumped in their midst, its palms balled
and eyes only half-shut. Shut for oblivion.
Too late to even try bringing him back around.
By now, it's been twelve hours since he
entered the room. When exactly he died
is anyone's guess. According to the man's brother,
who is later called in to identify the body,
he was the ED room as shelter from the April cold.
And still, no-one remembers actually
seeing him walk in. When I first heard this story,
I hoped it wasn't true, until a cursory glance
at each of that day's papers confirmed it.
There've been many stories and more yet to come,
but for him, at least, the worst is over.

Rooftop Blues

I could go for a quick smoke on the roof,
the steel vent pipe snaking
its lobed edges toward the window,
hear the incidental music of engines snarl up
from Richmond Street, relentless as diesel.
Maybe, just maybe, I see people for what we are
and want no part in it? Spilled lighter fluid,
a puddle of technicolor, swirls like marbled
paper where a lit match was dropped, and where
flames now spasm. A dove, olive branch
gripped in its beak, is shot down by tracer-bullet
in the lull of sundown, and, like me, bouncers
light up down laneways. Beats from a DJ throb
from an emergency exit to remind me that escape
is no longer possible, not now, then or ever,
and that I am moored, permanently, to here.

Sea State Martello

This span of bay is everywhere I look,
throbbing in heat, in kelp,
impossible to predict in its seasons.
Dawn is under way. But from my granite gunrest,
self-pitying and unshaven,
a prince without sire or dominion
eyes the silvered sea. Thunderheads
amass northward, like a long-
expected invasion that never arrived.

Tourists, in bowler hats and wielding canes,
make a June pilgrimage to my door.
They stand for free in the round room,
pay court to gas stove, iron bedstead,
their voices oiled with purblind quotation.
But my stone hears nothing, bar the tide-
boom drying in its crevice.
Day melts slowly back to dusk, sacrificial
and assured like an inquisitor's roar.

Only the Irish Sea is inbound: tanker
and yachts stagger on her waves' breaking
green, marked as the panther
and its sleeping pursuer.
It's a blessing to live with such nearness to
water. But neither you, nor I,
would dare call it 'neighbor'.
It's too noble for that, or any
other term of human endearment.

Below me are diving pools,
a stone's throw of steps, swimmers eeling in the noon-tide.
My aslant windows sip sunlight; night
lamps grapple with the shade. By the
lifeguard's hut, red flags flap
as if taunting the bull-headed sea.
A car ferry clears the harbour-mouth.

Home to amateur scholars and the eye-patched
crank who chose exile over the decorum
of classics, priestly sophism and opera-song,
I am a work of squat, defensive art,
cannon-proof and hounded by seagulls,
my throne the surf-bulleted rocks
whilst my flag, weary with weather,
lags in the grip
of dawn like a casualty.

Keep one eye seaward, always;
rain may muddy your sight like a blindfold.
Grey monsoons keep a civil distance.
But it is the destiny of monuments
to be toppled,
groundswells to engulf them.
So, from the imperial keystone,
windworn as parapets, the sea state may
now rise to meet me, a pale fever.

Devil Éire

... (la forme d'une ville
Change plus vite, hélas! que le coeur d'un mortel);
Baudelaire, 'Le Cigne'

I.
I'm on Grand Canal Bridge, watching fireworks ignite
the amber monolith of Google Docks, towering
over empty wharfs and warehouses at its feet;
from where I stand, I should probably be amazed
they're up for re-development at all: drydock and coalquay
bulldozed so trendy cafes and start-ups can be raised,
like keystones, in their place. But I don't see
the diggers or MEWPs, just the ashen pit where history
once stood. Developers mean to improve the city,
make it carbon to any other boomtown, smooth its rough
edges down, rebrand and gloss it over with LEDs, impose
Silicon Valley-imported values and applaud us
for deleting ours in the name of progress.
And sure, maybe it's all a necessary part of change: bulldoze
the place, re-forge it nice and new in steel and glass
and accessible only by keycard and passcode, future means.
I glimpse that future, in light of the fireworks.

II.
Late to rise, still bleary in last night's clothes,
Dublin at daybreak, LUAS halt-and-glide, real-time info.
Coffee gone stale while it's still hot, crushed close,
cheek by unshaven jowl jammed against a fogged window
as rush hour hits. Someone's phone is left on speaker,
earbuds crackle a Blindboy podcast as today's headlines
and weather are offhandedly scrolled. "Tickets there,
folks." Leap Card to hand, inspectors' machine dings
and a few fare dodgers leg it out of the rear tram
and the daily mantra—"change here for services
From Abbey Street"—*as Béarla agus as Gaeilge*
intones through, from Green Line to the Red, hisses
and the steel drag of tracks: mid-morning saga,

public sector or private gridlock, brass March burn,
commuter tangle, single journey or return.

III.
Lounging in stainless-steel chairs in the beer garden,
our rollies unlit, smooth-tongued sarcasm
soaks through the vast open plan all of a sudden.
Is it morally better to worship in the temple of capitalism
with a free gingham shopping tote, ATMs in every Spar?
Cashmere hoodies go for €220 a pop, a chalkboard
lurks outside Starbucks, and street art designed
to barely resemble graffiti glazes a restored
and refurbished pub wall. You say you don't mind
the preened beards and burritos, so let us erase the past,
forget its lessons. Anything repugnant to our sensibilities
can be denounced, banned; history can be revised,
rewritten in our own embalmed image. Eat cheese,
artisinal bread, and beetroot hummus, drink responsibly-
sourced ovo-lacto vegetarian cocktails. All it takes
is a leather-bound brunch menu to remind me I'm
neither alien nor native to curated and handcrafted cupcakes,
replete with 1,563 views and 400k likes on Instagram.

IV.
My liqueur is flavoured by region, by recipe. In rooms
made to resemble Parisian boudoirs, a fleck of amber
dims to crimson in my hand; leperous perfume,
lace masks and fire-breathers, band members
sawing through a sonata, and the honeyed orchids
all wither like leaves. Wine ages far better
than most people do, I'm told. Eager or timid,
I don't know which to be, as a parched and dim future
stares me in the eye. The Savoy's burgundy curtains
part, revealing yet another overhyped spectacle
in hi-res, and we continue to scroll vacantly
through our newsfeeds as rust sweeps over it all.
Shadows blot us easily out of our integrity,
our baseline softened from years of indulgence.
And there is much on offer at inflated prices,

but something has surely been lost, perhaps forever,
or at least, priced out. If we're to call that progress,
then I'll be much happier staying out here.

V.
The Vive headset strapped to my cranium, the sensor
Morphs and enhances my vision to luminous 3-D,
Scanning my brain as zen colours swirled.
Before long, I was on a mission of lurid graphics,
Moving as if underwater, clutching the controller
Like rosary beads. Out of this world, on a mine
Cart rollercoaster, the vertigo got me as I
Swerved from side to side and was catapulted through
Lava pits, gorges, snow-dusted peaks in LED,
And always on the verge of derailing.
I forget how long I was immersed, how out of reach
I became to everyone—
Still seated where I was when I began. Each
Thought was recorded. Passwords grant me access.

VI.
Sure look, as the fella says, success has many fathers,
but failure's a bastard. Yet the future's improvised
after all, and in good time, wouldn't you rather
see the country fast-forward into a paradise
manufactured and sponsored by the algorithmic rust
of fake news, Twitter spats, trolls, selfie queens,
hashtags, well-signalled virtue, all your airbrushed
hallucinations fed interminably to you on ink-black screens?
Gulp down that daily outrage fueling your FOMO
in paper-flower sprays, floods of crocodile
tears retched from the stony nimbus cloud; and keep
acting like you're beyond the reach of social
media influence and clickbait adverts, how steeped
you are in the doctrines from which you can't untangle.
VII.
Everything's visible in a glass museum of surveillance—
drones patrolling the clouds to scan a dim laneway
in 8K for the Garda Air Support Unit, each wingspan

trimmed and sheared like a vulture fund;
the rain, sweating out the last of its acid reflux,
rubs it all down, tattooing teardrops on every face
for infrared satellites to finally recognize.
Solar panels wink at the sky, glazed and on-trend
above the towpath. The suspiciously-angled cursor
of this device transmits my mind back to Google
HQ, boasting the world's most diverse workforce
with the most regimented of goals.
Will paymaster make a colony of this place again,
price the rest of us out of their market research
that will see our economy thawed, as seagulls
squawk like data updates and entire families lurch
from hotel to garda station and back to street again?
But sure, we're fine with it, happy, in fact, to relinquish
our privacy if it means the chaos won't touch us
in the end. Cables are reprogrammed, planted below
soil and interred in concrete; soon they will tangle
together, like hoarfrost licking a DART window as it
hurdles past the gasworks' cast-iron skeleton, now
an apartment building with antique fixings,
cauterised by winter's slow blowtorch. This island
is nothing but a haven of low-hanging taxes,
ensuring their profits aren't distributed anywhere
else, and the lens boasts a view of the glass-jawed city—
the omnipresent logo, rain on stainless-steel windows,
how inescapable it all is, a CCTV's unblinking eye.

VIII.
To be honest, I don't actually mind the jade reflective
skylights and atriums that much. Tell you one thing,
if the sludgy basin of a Norse dockside paved
with tarmac, the solid white stripes of bus lanes,
flash of taxi sign and rush-hour engines chattering
like pebbles in backwash, a red light's halt
and the go-ahead of green, was to be resurrected,
I'm not sure if I'd applaud or decry its arrival.
But what of the future? Surely the past has been lingered
upon for long enough, and the city must endure

without the hands that built it or the hands that
refined it at civic orders. God only knows and perhaps
only God should know, as monuments crumble
and the glass spires keep rising, from sloped
swamp to crystal skyline, as we vanish into the cinders
of history, like starships through the galaxy.

IX.
Even as she zeroes the selfie stick in, her face
is turned downward, pose struck half-heartedly,
filter selected, makeup left half-done, eyes
suddenly averted, like a pair of sleeping larvae.
She pushes her head forward, blithe and giggling
for the split second when the click is pressed,
takes several more 'til the perfect shot is taken,
captioned, hashtagged, and posted.
The angle's good, light gores through blemish
and crease; but I know better than to look
too closely at this newly-created memory
enshrined forever on her profile, as like after
like pile up like burnt offerings to her flesh,
and she is sorry that I can see her.

X.
Rage Against the Machine played there once, back in
'93; Jeff Buckley, too. Now it's demolished, replaced
by yet another Maldron or Jury's Inn
or one-euro shop, faceless, drab, disgraced.
I used to go there for the club nights: hazy memories
of midnight gigs, 4-deck techno, a rare acoustic set
from Damo, belters spilling out to the side alleys.
Today, there's only sky, bulldozers in silhouette;
no matter for the yearly-elected cabals who misgive
and sign deeds too fast to even allow for memory
as they revere dead icons, ignore those that still live.
Another great venue razed, or left on shaky ground.
"Is this not the city of poets and singers?" It used to be,
friend, but, sure look. Aren't we quick to let them drown?

Rope Jockey

A text from the agency tells me
when and where to be
and what tools to have on-site
(though I know that already):
harness and gloves, high-viz
and hard hat. On the Luas,
I watch Dublin hunker in March rain,
her blue-black skyline tightened like a toolbelt
and head into the site at 7 on the dot,
with an Americano
from Frank and Honest
and a heart attack sandwich
(that's a breakfast roll to you)
to keep me going.
The site is knotted, impassable as a jungle:
a cluster of skeletal cranes loom
in the sky, statically iron,
set in stone or steel, balanced against all weather,
jibs shredding cloud as the wind's high grip
rattles through bony lattice
and chain-sling as they slowly swivel
to lift granite slabs to the roof:
pulleys and outriggers and bolts set in a concrete base,
concrete vomited from mixers, giant rust-
scuffed boxes stacked high
with rollers and chains, corrugated ridges.
I wonder how soon it'll be
before funding gets pulled and it's left derelict,
not even a quarter of the way finished:
the rich weight of industry, injurious as scorn.
Secretly, I'm grateful for the job,
that I get to work on this building
destined to be a hotel
or some tech firm's HQ,
I.D. card swinging and bleeping me in,
my serial number memorized like girl's name.
Rung by rung, I climb

as if towards heaven, past girders and I-beams
slung low in ruled, russet mesh,
my wings soaked in caffeine and blood,
numb to the view of Dublin
nestling far below me, steel-grey morass
of roofs and webbed pavements, traffic
an arterial drip-feed. I sit in the cab controls
like a pilot becalmed in mid-air,
grip the levers and maneuver the crane into life,
harnessing it to come 'round full circle,
as if in slow motion
with a conclusive thud. Load follows load,
lb follows lb, and I'll do
as many as thirty, forty lifts a day
if I have to, the back jib
and counterweight locked in their waltz,
'til a voice on the radio confirms:
"Yeh, she's all clear, boss."
And time isn't measured by my watch
but by the rise and sink of the sun,
a solar disk in tiled and black in slow hurtle
across the glass cages,
reddening my face by degrees. It's mad
how dark it gets in the space of a few hours,
how much the city looks like a crime scene,
how unstoppable it all seems.

Mountpleasant Aubade

'That's too noble a word. Love. It's not for the likes of us.'
—Henning Mankell, *Mördare utan ansikte*

Call it a healthy disrespect for money—the holes burnt
in your pocket, coins and Leap Card to hand, coffee
leeched of flavor, bills clogging the postbox,
your ritual of dry shampoo and blush at the hall mirror,
hair bobby-pinned, keys bunched on the table
with the rest of your small necessities. Through the ceiling,
the footsteps of the couple living above us wake you;
grudgingly, we hoist roller blinds to meet the sun's polar
clarity. Where we live, landlords charge 500 squids just
to view a property. We're lucky to be where we are, I suppose.
Down the street, our more well-off neighbors
flaunt their employees through half shut windows.
Everyone else walks, resigned, dogged, to work;
it's how we live in the shadow of something,
insufficient funds, rent increase. Threat of eviction.
All morning, I'll watch you climb out of your pit
of sleep, your blouse unbuttoned, skirt unzipped, a Xanax
setting you quietly adrift. Metallic clouds waft over
as we walk into work; the city clears its throat around us,
wind shakes beads of acid from branches, you go your
way, I go mine at the College Street traffic lights.
What'll it be, so? Asleep on your morning commute, ash
filling your mouth, fire-seeds for breakfast, savage to the taste?
Or else the minted air, cooling you to radiance?

Sea Batteries

Sea Batteries

This harbor wall is truer than any god,
chequered rust glazing fuse-blasted stone.

The sea thunders over and over, between
north-easterly choirs and abrasive granite.

For now, though, there's a lull in the fighting
between wave and wall, the light of June

smearing itself over horned rocks. I ask
myself, how many navvies poured their lives

into stone, just to build these pincer-piers,
carving the slowest of inroads on the tide,

iron cables sagging to the water's edge?
A thousand men, maybe more, who sweated

for asylum, hauling tallow-greased drays
from the Dalkey pits, laden with the import

of granite and the friction of their hands.
If there is anything to love about the place,

it's the closeness of the sea, the tide's
ebbing murmur, the waves' crumbling chant,

miniature forests of algae swaying underwater.
The bandstand, with rust-tattooed masonry,

letting the rain enter as lazily as the sun.
A catamaran throbs whitely on the horizon,

towing behind her a chain of swollen miles,
the mould of her prow acute as a whetstone.

Even now, under a crash of spray, I ask:
does the harbor hold any provision for exiles?

Oar

Goring the guts of a wave, the rocky outcrop
squats in a pooling flow, jagged and iron-grey.
The promontory stands taller than any mast.
I feel my lungs scorched by paper-thin air,
luminous breath spilling into oblivion, boots
crunched by piled stone, and soak of rain
through my oilskins. My barnacle-coated oar
is to be taken from the thwart and shouldered inland,
up the shingly pass, scrub plain and underbrush,
until I reach the bald clifftop where a fleet of cormorants
reel, and the sea chafes the ear only in whispers.
The peace I was promised is to be found there.

Immramm

Mark you Brendan, reefing oxhide sails,
The currach veering broadside on,
The glutted fish all ears as he preaches
Over the hiss of breakers.

The sun advances its brass doldrum.
An ember-eyed devil squats on the prow,
Its tongue a meatless fork
And psalmody its frozen repellant.

Mark you Brendan, his name loved
By manuscripts and whorled icons,
Clutching the groaning halyard,
The sea his punishment and his promise.

The sails shiver. The oars prod a humpback
Islet, shaggy with the green of algae.
It rears heavily and sinks in white seizure.
A following wind dives low, interring

The boat's flaxen chassis
In and among the grey fathoms,
Smoked waves bloodying
Her hull in a shower of sparks.

So mark you Brendan, cataracts
Of salt jabbing nostril and eyelid,
A rusty halo now his bearing,
The Eden-shore in his exhausted sight.

Bádóirí*

Caithfidh an fharraige a chuid féin a fháil†
—Gaelic proverb.

Connemara terns plumb the wild surface

quarrying for mackerel in icy deepwater.
The tourist season is winding down; nervous,
tacking, a yacht glides out of Roundstone Harbour
for the night, stiff crosswinds jangling her gasket,
alert for rocks, tidemarks, or a spiked shift in the calm.
Refuge isn't to be found on the Great Blasket
or Inishkea, mercy pending in the palm
of providence's hand. Tarred maroon sails dapple
the cove, cut finer than hemp. Forebears implant
a practise that modernity may never drown, in chapel
and boatyard, to bear the surf's hissing filament.
Spiddal jetty, fogged as a beached hulk,
lets the lash of their headfast in, a wake's white signature
blurring the upsurge's line, hollow keels to caulk
with pitch and moss. Puzzling sheets of gossamer
mist steam over mountain and sea. Peace and love
are words to be scoffed at; skill holds all the value.
Hard as the nails driven home amid strakes, they hove
to in October dusk, veteran single-handed crew,
their leathery backs turned on bogland and field
for the sake of wind-rattled seas, stone-choked shores,
the cut and clamour of craft, oak-ribbed and sealed,
staunch timbers to creak the course.
Led by the boom's high-flying shaft, they buck
savagely on a rip current, robbed of sleep, a haul
of bodies stewing coldly amidships. Neither luck
nor lenience shore them; the foghorn's grunt, a full-
toned animus for the shade, rumbles over the bay
each hour, the last sound to seal up the ear
along the gurgling lullaby of a rogue wave,
high and dry in a sou'wester's icy crosshair.

The boats have grown old with a grace that they,
the makers, can no longer recognise.
So let day end and dusk thrive with the tidemark;
let the shells whisper of storms in shingly vowels
when tentacled kelp is brought in to sell.
This is the wild Atlantic way, tempting to the stranger
who lacks the inborn grit to sail the sea
but not the frightened awe to admire it,
who hikes its wind-dry cliffs in order to catch
a glimpse of arched sails and flailing masts
careening the wet burden, and snaps the grey eddy
thrashing and coming about on spluttered ebbs.
For the bádóirí, a harbour is a proven miracle.
Turns are taken on the tiller; they shoot out nets
as if to haul immortality from the pouring backwash.
Quayside and oar bear out the briny crash.

*Literally, boatmen or boat-masters.

†'The sea will always take its full portion'.

Rescue 116

I listen to the audio
of their last known signal,

moored to the headline by the
morbid lure of my curiosity:

breathless and crackly,
the wind a surging screech

above helicopter blades, as the Atlantic
foams and flexes like a cruel muscle,
the lingo of danger, co-ordinates of surf

and swell as it pitches, veering to starboard
of the lighthouse, on its perch of blistering
herpetic granite, as it blinks back rain,

the distress call guzzling down saltwater
and cut terminally off,

their drowned voices
a chorus for help.

The Signal Fire

For Larry Hanlon, former lighthouse tender

At seventy, you re-light the signal fire. Your eye
Drinks down the horizon, the solid horizon
That no hurricane can smash or sink:
Scarred reefs, blurring fog, drowned sandbars,
Strands crooked as a corsair's smile;
A parade of lighthouses, slicing open the dark.

What point, what purpose do they now serve
Except as fodder for a day-tripper's Instagram
Feed? Breakers claw at each foreshore, upswells
Of running spray slosh and slop the fixed flame
That blazes above a crested zone in knells.
But peer offshore, to where shipping lanes swerve

In and out: see the shoal-struck buoys bob and blink
Mutually, bulk carriers lying anchored
In wait for a tide-turn, glad for that timed wink
Divulged on the AIS's unbiased signal. Blurred,
Unformed, darkness heaves into view,
Adrift on the sea's abyssal face, that a constellation

Of beacons shall pierce: Poolbeg. Kish. Hook Head.
Baily. Rockabill. Fastnet. Malin. Beacons
Of service, founded in concrete. Glassy, coaxial
Eyes ignite every five seconds, an intended mercy:
All of them and more you helped fuel, thrill
Of your odyssey undergone in the world's flooded

Corner. Each was someone's home once, as well
As a pledged outpost, the light raking the deep in chaos
Or calm, its solar radiance, holding clockwork vigil
On sunken cliffs, the rust-daubed rail of the terrace
Assuring that you are almost there, port is in sight,
You are safe now, you shall have shelter soon.

So set a course beyond their reach, beyond ocean—
Bruise walloping the bay, beyond skies peppered by stars,
For we are now gathered to celebrate you, to bask
In your aged radiance, to keep the flame
Of your seven-decade adventure burning on,
Undimmed, uneroded by the tsunami of years.

Carrier

Aircraft carrier USS John F Kennedy in Dublin Bay, May, 1996

F-14s revved for take-off on the air wing.
Jet fuel stung my nose from a good mile away—
Outsize quarantine kept her utmost as a spider.
Strafed by her bow wave, lashings of spray
Slopped the East Pier. The sun was in my eyes,
But I think I saw motley bunting ruffle her radar
Dish fore and aft, fiesta caching her reactor.

With her godlike turbines and barbed antenna she
Lurked to port, far from the Virginia shipyard where
Her keel was first laid to carve Persian Gulf swells,
The anchor burst to surface, hooks spread like a martyr.
Was that the calm that heralds or follows a storm?
The bay stung by its own tail, red waterline, white propulsion,
Blue hangar, typhoons anchored in silent proximity?

The Long Watch

i.m. Irish sailors lost at sea during 'the Long Watch' of WWII.

For Eamon Mag Uidhir

U-boats ranging the sea-trench had us marked;
a destroyer on passage from Portsmouth swiveled
its turret in our direction.

Most unsplendid isolation—our discreet Emergency:
government rations wolfed down with livid urgency,

the country once more in danger of starvation.
Men risked the all-clear of magnetic mines,
torpedoes puncturing supply lines

aboard nearly-new colliers and steam packets,
each named after trees, 'EIRE' tarred port

and starboard, their hulls brittle as neutrality.
What service, what grit: to willingly barter a life
deep-sixed below sea level in an engine-room

while surf sloshed fantails, oil fizzed past midnight,
and no navy lads left to drown, not on our bosun's watch,

anyway: Axis or Allied, shivering and soaked in confusions
of surf—an SOS flare needed no translation.
We'd haul them from the froth without hesitation.

On deck, the bronchial stack smoked a final signal
as MG 17's spluttered, spat from overhead—

fiery gougings through plate-iron, bloodied
life vests clogging every ebb and crest. Essential
demand, manifest supply, green global stretch:

all sunk without trace, or else washed up on beaches.

Maude Jane Delap

Where cold-water coral crouches
in the undertow of Valentia
and the seal chirps and slouches
despite a gannet's diving caw,
she rows among grey-green swells.
Lunar plankton-glow frisks
the skeg, a crest's rogue gurgle
and sunken tow-net whisk

the sea with their crimped scrape.
Humming to herself hymns soft
as the noted and nameless kelp,
she sets all fear, all doubt adrift
like the plunked mutter of stones,
works her passage to rarer knowledge.
Fathoms drink her dropped line
'til a swarm of jellyfish are dredged

like pearls for pruning, to be ferried
inshore to her crude herbarium,
where possibility shimmers amid
the squelching dreg of a storm.
So salute her skull's basin
where theories stealthily swim
and test against the current,
wrenching as the sight and smell

of sea-spray gusting over the bow.
She has filed away the waves' murk
and dove headlong to get through
a natural banquet, beard of rock,
tide-splash, shingle-clack underfoot,
to know that Whitestrand is combed
enough as she disembarks, alights
for the luminance of her lab's sanctum.

John de Courcy Ireland

Ma quando disse: "Lascia lui, e varca,
che qui e buon con la vela e coi remi
quantunque puo ciascun, pinger sua barca;
            —Dante, *Purgatorio, Canto* 12, lines 4-6

Yours was the first low cadence of tides,
A rusted bawley now sent to the breakers. Who
Could follow you through soused everglades,
Your phantom still set on cataloguing the slew
    Of uncharted alts, death-crooning mermaids?

And now the salty wonder-pill pushes away
The database of names you'd so fussily gathered,
Registries of men scuttled and unsung, the etymology
Of barnacled weather-rail and waving oleander,
    The cut-glass Atlantic, washed fodder for history.

You organised Dun Laoghaire lifeboat station
Like a man aloft, standing watch for a glimpse
Of reef or risk, good and lost in the mirror-like ocean
Whose urges you knew to exalt. The oily lamps
    Kindle half-measured miles, inked into a margin

Of your silver memory. This pebbly ledge
Whitens at dusk. The oarlock's twirling glance
Acts on your hand's biding, your penultimate voyage
Too far off for gales to gag your response
    To our common and ignored heritage.

We islanders, oblivious to the cold blue element
That is needed and fuels our need, have dove
Past the porpoise's inshore library, the green ferment
    In an appendix of anemone, a luminous sea-cave

Immersed in plain-texts of sand, the acrostic hunt
For bass or mackerel flavouring our hook.
Your headstone, if you had one, would face the coast
    As pilgrims face Mecca, no matter how deeply brooked,

How deeply moored in soil you'd be. An offshore gust,
Hard as the fact, bestows on us neither a look-
Out's clarity nor strength enough to bear
The burden forecast or the grey churn
Of a maelstrom, our blindness made clear
To the global sea that binds nation to nation,

As you had always declared.
Your Vico Road bristles with uncut cypresses
And her dissolving sky, with scuppers of cloud,
Rams the rolling swish that calmed you, redresses
An anchor feted with the shame of rust and seaweed.
You are bound homeward, yet willing your mind always
To frigid depths where prosperity may be trawled.

Sandeel Bay

Sandeel Bay is deserted in the morning,
No ships blur the horizon.
No rust-red umbrae, uncaring as stone,
Mirror the sky's oxblood warning.

But the squall waits, infusing as before.
Today, I approach with a new cigarette,
My shadow coiled in a brackish net,
Eyes dimmed by the asphaltic shore.

For I know the stars will pause and pulse,
The freak waves' crystal momentum
Will drown Sandeel like a triturated victim,
If ever myself or my song prove false.

Granuaile

For Niamh Keoghan

Atlantic swells are my surging heritage;
Limpet and barnacle cling to my back.

I know the water like my own unshackled mind,
Jetsam sprawling in the surf with luminous fatigue.

I have told my people not to pray for me:
Only the wind and tide may bless my voyage.

The deck of my caravel is drenched in salt—
My youngest son was born aboard ship.

From the prow, I see my world for the first time:
Clew Bay echoing with a gull's strident vow,

Currachs dredging the inlet for herring or haddock,
Clare Island besieged by hurdling waves.

Signal fires twist and turn over Rockfleet, insolent
And primed as the guns we fire on any ship

That dares make inroads on our serene cove.
In gentle weather, when the sea simmers down,

I forget the waves' frothy bile, Spanish sailors, dregs
Of the Armada, butchered en masse on our sand,

Their blood ripening this country's withered soil,
While adventure's afterglow perishes amid the kelp.

My crew never sing chanteys when hoisting sail;
The high winds are music enough for them.

They rally to me as they rally rudder and sweep,
Heeding my commands like oceanic law.

Their name for me is the Sea-Queen of Connaught,
Beautiful for the danger I pose to wayfarers.

My ghost will never settle for a wooden cage.
Tell my people not to pray for my memory.

Tell them no more blood may be spilled for mine.
Tell them I belong, as I always have, to the sea.

Navigator

After dusk, I rely on the stars,
keeping watch from the wheelhouse
to gauge our clear-cut position.
Luminous barnacles cling to the sky.
Like a weightless megalith
left by a primeval, the ship glides steadily,
all lamps lit, a halcyon breeze whispering
through her rigging and side scuttles
like a consecration.
I mark the moon's polar glow,
my pencil's frantic scrape
scuffing the logbook.
The gentle science of stargazing:
even at their incredible distance
undaunted by the iron laws of gale
and cross-current, a trinity or quartet
of stars will set a clear reckoning for us.
The pilot steers the miles we sought,
our anchor is dropped a mile offshore.
O stars, burnished for rovers,
point us home in the drizzly shade:
let our song be no forlorn outcry to you.

Achaemenides

The sybils didn't bother with me
but one or two poets filled the blanks in:
an Ithakan king, vying for the sea,
conscripted men to the mast on
his flagship crossing to Troy.
Nearly his whole crew, wretched cost
of rudderless roving, would die
in some way or another. I'd outlast

my comrades, my skull a cave
for every marooned thought,
cleared by sea-winds. The waves'
aged murmur, a wine-dark clot
of spray, was my eternal clock
to flail and flare on the ebb.
I stood watch as if on my ship's deck
and slept in a berry-shrub

at night, held my hungry peace.
He was out there, tremoring the island
with his rams, roaring without cease,
a brute, drooling shepherd, blind
in one gored eye and still raging.
Him, and a tribe of him, their fangs
gritted by quotidian corpse-chewing,
eyes rusted as mooring rings.

I'd neither the brains nor the backbone
to engineer my escape, as my pilot
had. I preferred to linger, my beard laden
with barnacles, and eye the blood-lit
skyline for rescue. Laughing gulls,
black-armoured scorpions and flame-
petalled flowers thronged the hills
and shore, and the sun's daily whim

beat too heavily for comfort. When

sleep did take me, I saw brass shields,
chariots, my old xiphos drawn,
flames tearing through Trojan fields.
I prayed for the gods to be cruelly kind
and smite me with flood or drought;
somehow I kept my presence of mind,
did not gasp my despair out.

I needed a woman, needed her touch
and kiss. I thought often of the girls
I'd loved before sailing, memories a crutch
for my mind to stoop on. Heavy scrolls
of loneliness, heat-rippled, tore at me.
I'd see none of them again, I knew,
had drunk my life's fill of their beauty;
and lost them like my ill-starred crew.

If I am to die, may it be by man's
hand, not crushed or sunk or devoured.
I prayed for that much, at least: the plans
of Olympus to see me safely delivered
from his eyeball's crimson gush,
the cave we'd made our woollen escape
from gawking at the bay, lethal hush
stirring him from sleep, the grapes

that gave him his wine burst in his palm,
his voice and footfall alike echoing
the strafed harmonic of thunder. Blessed to swim,
or condemned to sink: I'd no way of knowing
until a fresh, high glut of tide brought
the Dardanian galleys, and my first glimpse
of raised sails, bellying and white,
in an age. Mariners walked in slumps,

leaning to their oars, arid lips
panting for haven and home, beards
surf-smeared, fibrous as bullwhips.
I saw horsehair helms and blunt swords,

a fleet steered clear off the map's edge
and held back, afraid for my life.
But these were men in the anchorage,
not beasts. Surely blood was enough

for mercy; with my thorn-fixed cloak,
what possible threat was I to them now?
Despair, weariness, terror and shock
felled me at the knee, and I howled out:
"Men of Troy, fly you far from this shore!
Where you make port is not important.
The danger you here face is too great to ignore.
Put back to sea, save yourselves this instant!

I who was your Grecian foe, now beg thee
to grant but one meagre service:
bring me with you if you will, or else kill me!
But cast off now, before the giants arise!"
I say this without shame: I wept, groveled,
kissed the barren sand before them.
The oldest of them stepped forward
to give me his hand, and I stood abeam.

Their captain, a born survivor as mine
once was, saw the giant for himself
and did not stay to fight. Jaded as his men
were, he led them back down the pebbly shelf
to the ships, with myself in their number,
and we slipped a swift course from the cove.
The one-eyed clan cursed our venture
but fathoms ran too deep for their heave,

their stride. Now seaborne and free at last,
I was ragged locus for the shoal
and river-mouth, reefs clenched like a fist
under the bare walls of the Geloan.
Yet, sun-drunk and hunger-shredded,
I saw we had a good skipper, wary
in his pilotage but alert to the dreaded

unfolding of a voyage, dogged emissary

for nomads. Yet he never claimed
to know his heading; he was as lost as I.
As gratitude, I kept my head down
and worked the mains, my new duty
to share utterly in my rescuers' fate.
They fed me, healed me, found me a home.
And it came as no surprise of late
that a price isn't on my head, or that no-

one even set off in search of me
or my brothers. Yet I am here, thankful
and restored, saved by an enemy
whom I greet and look to now as an idol
of my flight, no longer hunched
as the rock I saw the blind herder fling
at my receding ship. So from staunch
shores, now, may my voice once more sing.

In Virgil and Ovid, the Greek castaway Achaemenides is a member of Ulysses' crew who is left stranded on the island of the Cyclopes after his comrades make their escape. He lives on in the hills until he is eventually rescued by Aeneas, who is seeking a new homeland following Troy's destruction at the hands of the Greeks.

Passage Plan

Anchor of yearning,
Chain me to the seabed
Where boneless algae stands upright.
If the breakers grow fat on kelp,
Then let me sleep among the drowned.

Keel of tenacity,
Propel me through this saw-like cove
Before drowned sorrows resurface,
Oily as tentacles,
Intent on dragging our frail craft under.

Bowsprit of fealty,
Lash my limbs to the figurehead
When green salt spices the deck
And no terra firma stands in sacred sight,
That I may face the wind's crescendo.

Yard-arm of solicitude,
Poise me above board, over the gulf
That an iron prayer may be offered
For this uncalled ship
To land at safer shores.

Breath

On a talon-cragged hot spring shore,
the steel kiss of a daybreak wave lasts too long
for hard-won judgment, threats and curtains
of rain snarl under a loud August wind, away
from tourists charter-fishing aboard a varnished gulet.
The surf cradles your limbs like ballast.

From the hotel jetty, out on grey riptides
there drifts a punctured dinghy,
a cipher in the Aegean
under a roughshod moon, with gnarled lifejackets
and rucksacks over the side, its motor long dead.

Your sunken eyes close on the black groundswell.
A fever, rabid, seismic, waxes the waves, white
morsels of surf cannonade sandbar and shoal.
Ocean is bartering back kelp, carnage-red jetsam
and an infant's corpse, washed up on the beach.

I can see the tide massaging your back
as if such a barnacled simulation of mercy
could deliver you from the whitecaps
that tossed the raft you crouched in over
before pressing you face-down to the sand,
the channel's cold slop brimming
to your marrowbones, gutting your spongy
life vest, draining suds from your mouth,
profuse and unaided as smoke.

You are becalmed now, in your dampest zone—
cool is the water, and sick to the pit of its stomach
for exempting you from its mercy,
unalert to the glib tears which will anoint you
now that the world witnesses your sinking.

At the border, arrests sprout like tumours.

All is on the hook. The brine buffs shaded stone,
deckchairs take cover under parasols at water's edge.
You lie in still-warm state, respiring for a pocket of air
that can no longer grant you the mercy of breath.

*This poem is dedicated to the victims of the Syrian refugee crisis and to their
survivors.

Bearings

I am the tobacco soiling a sailor's teeth,
the first gulp of firewater to singe his craw.

Beholden to neither figurehead nor decree,
the sea is its own empire, its own palpable law.

I am the slow plunge of a salver's periscope,
the cryptic cavern vomiting aqueous surf like milk

while salt water lazily scrubs at your toes,
windless doldrums lie too clean full to caulk.

When you trip in rock-pools, snorkel for oysters,
or snag raw mussels to be eaten onshore,

remember me, your island republic, estranged
from the sea as islands are from one another.

I am the shelter you'd much prefer to freedom,
the weather eye piercing latitude and departure

I am the unspread word, the cave bird,
hum of a conch when you raise it to your ear

I am the closest many have ever gotten to a saga,
the grey lull seeping from a hurricane's breast

I am the sudden power cut in radars and VHF,
a storm-surge promised in a Met Eireann forecast.

I am the benediction uttered for smooth sailing,
soaked in despair and maddeningly stale

I am one more hump of granite burst from the sea;
like barnacles to a keel, your myths affixed to me.

The Liner Reina Del Pacifico during Sea Trials

The North Channel, September 11th, 1947

Like a beast's airless belly, the *Reina's* charred stokehold,
a heat-slurred pyre weaving oil-mist to lagan—
one more fraught ship of a fraught state.
Her gutted crankshafts boom in sight and mind
scattering like motorized fanfare
all the way across the North Channel to Harland's.

The native gantries, poised as if forever
above Belfast's graving docks, stand quiet as a tug
eases her upriver, a day after the fact. On slipway
and wharf, yardmen pause at their work,
doffing dunchers in sober respect
for the newly dead and their ill-starred liner;
silence briefly rules the deafening shipyard.

*

The war ended two years ago. Union flags fly
at dutiful half-mast, drum and fife bang to tribal tempos,
a sash of loyal flame fastens the city in two.
Lives are ruled by iron, the discordant opera of hammer
banging off plate, crane sirens blaring on the Lough.
In that Mecca of smoker's cough and craftsmanship,
1, 742 sturdy keels are laid all under
the foreman's scowl, and a shared Woodbine.

Work snowballs. Vessels that saw service in war
return to their old functions, troopships converted
back to liners, as if trauma can be so easily shaken off
by a metal refit. Mild September: that it's a day
eminently suitable for sea trials cannot be contested.
Once more, *Reina del Pacifico*, aged but still
with plenty of horsepower left in her, will ferry
tourists to Latin America by way of Merseyside,

authorized for a full capacity of 886 passengers,
powered on hydrocarbons.
                              A floating shit-heap
in her war years, she's a great white titan again,
one of Belfast's proudest. Deep-water oblivion
and failure in the bearings cross only the minds
                              of naysayers.
Yet, in sight of the shore, roughly seven miles off
Copeland, raven-black smog gusts from her rear funnel.
Overheating in her crank chamber has caused all four
engines to explode, killing twenty-eight of her crew.
Truly a perilous line of work to be in, not a vocation.
The accident seemed—and it is no exaggeration
*Of language—just impossible, but it happened.**

                              *

Measuring her miles in the Firth of Clyde
away from the torrid sea—
full ahead, dead slow, half astern, stop.
After today, she'll be called a "hoodoo ship"—a vessel
with bad luck riveted into her inboard and plating,
her name a cautionary tale for marine engineers.

The escape hatch gapes, open as a secret:
her engine room's mined penetralia is more sewer
than the motor auxiliary of a working ship, and a soon-
to-be luxury liner at that. A half-lit trove of arithmetical
valves, control levers and shafts, where men are gathered,
caked in dust, boosted on stale, whiskey-laced coffee…
                              doing what, exactly?

Talking football, or shop? Slagging each other off
or else getting to it? Grumbling a work-song
in flat unison, sweat oozing steadily on each brow
                    as they brake the propeller shaft?

Brothers, boyfriends, husbands, sons, sons-in-law,
fitters, draughtsman, engineers, superintendents,

chancers, drinkers, card players, amateur footballers—
                    soon-to-be-corpses—
each with a bone in his teeth for the job ahead.
The motor thrums metrically above them. Shovels blunt
and the fire room is seldom breached by daylight,
only the pistons' fiendish glow for visibility—
                    panelboards wire a crackly

transmission of hazard and hard labour, reeking
of diesel and atomised air. It comes without warning.

A roar of glass shatters the routine, louder than the crunch
of a rudder touching the water for the first time.
The men feel only the oil's toxic blast gorging
on their jaws and sinews, flames dancing like locusts
over heavy boiler suits, the smoke's acrid perfume
swirling to their lungs, drowning screams in black
overkill, its full thickness singeing them to cadavers.
One writhes through the doorway of the water room
like an effigy made sentient, his body engulfed,
embers licking at his sleeve and eye, and another
is crushed under a buckled stairwell, his wheezes stifled.

Some die instantly, while others have five more days
to go before succumbing to their blisters. The rest
lie choked and stewed beneath burst pipes and lumps
of steel in the flammable slurry, luminous spurts
of arcing from where a light exploded in its fixture.
Oil gushes contentedly as blood or mercy.
They can wait only for rescue or death now.

                              *

In Belfast, ghosts shuffle among dockside sheds
toward the Queen's Island, nurtured
from briny slag and sediment
beyond steel plating, beyond ice-clause.
Oily soot-stains on the funnel are the sole proof
of an explosion ever taking place

aboard the Reina del Pacifico.
Work, wages, shipboard politics, all up in smoke.
A cigarette case,
stamped with the ship's name and image,
is dropped over the side
and down below, the engine room seethes
like the belly of a whale
wherein a man may find himself swallowed.
The ghosts loiter in the fog.
Freshly-cut flames ripple to their cores.

A Volunteer

I've only ten minutes to myself in the station,
Ten precious minutes to get my head clear.
Sable curtains of rain bleed over the pier
Like a challenge, hazing the peninsula.
Between gulps of coffee, I take off my boots
To remind myself of yesterday's duties
And yesterday's drowned. Soon, the others
Will arrive at a radio's bidding and together
We'll shoulder the boat down the slipway,

Our delta sign hissed stiffly behind teeth,
Our bearings not yet taken on the sea's
White scrum. Every time we motor out
Into the bay, I pray for this to not be my final
      Boat duty. We plod along
At ten knots, helmeted and life-jacketed

Against switchblade-rapid westerlies,
The outboard motor swamped in spray
A blur of waves lashing the gunwale
With dark unbidden virulence, until we
Round the cove rocks, doleful as tobacco
In steep surf-siege, and see the first stricken
      Swimmers, crazed and afloat,
Or just static in the water.

It's then I start to crave the thrill of salt
Bailing into my blood, tunnelling
My vision and stinging it clean. For let it be
Known, the quiet swimmers are the ones
To really worry about, since they never flail
Or shriek for help in the telluric current,
As the movies might have you believe. It feels
Like forever, asking them if they're alright.

The faces of the drowned get harder to read.
Are they the debt owed to these roaring swells?

Are they the unavoidable due
Set in something other than stone,
Binding oaths in the thickness of blood?
And are we, their rescuers, the ones to pay it?

For the ones still breathing, I want neither praise
Nor thanks—just the certitude
Of their leeway from deepening water.

Salvors' Reach

In response to Baudelaire's 'L'Homme et la mer'.

No, not brothers, or even foes, but dependants,
And even then, certainly not forever. For some,
Ocean is a sleepless mirror to be overcome
Or stilled. Grey-green sluices surge in segments,

Inky calm roils back the tide. The sunken heart
And dredged soul, both locked to its labour,
Confound it for a gold-stashing neighbour,
Sea-traffic tossed long as litanies on a chart.

Chasmal master and fleshy slave, ill-at-ease
With clumps of bronze kelp tonguing the brine
Like smugglers, murky as a plunged bloodline.
It does not serve our soft-focus chanteys,

Stoked by rhythm. Beyond the salvors' reach,
Strapwork smearing rust over its agate-
Strung lunalae, reef-grooved, waves set
To rattle stones with the suck of their drainage,

The calm they bring to us illusory and brief.
Mercy is small here. Fog, hellish spurts of rain,
Make its drive of death knowable and akin
To the hearts of men. Or, so you wish to believe.

Man is a tourniquet for leechings of harmony,
A windbound anchor clinching the basalt.
His works are swallowed by the cold rise of the sea.
The upsurge brims, crashing to a halt.

Borders

On the Shooting of Lyra McKee in Derry

After John Milton

So, do we avenge the murals and saintly bones
scattered over Creggan streets, with cold
intent of gunmetal where soldiers once patrolled,
molten sparks to scrape stop signs, traffic cones,
police Land Rovers, petrol-scorched air? Stones
to step over, keep her in mind: a reporter on hold.
No-one declared this ground as sacred, or refueled
it for us to strike matches, hold up our phones
and record her last moments before a stray
bullet took her, as sirens, lurid ingots aglow
with sodium, cruised through the dark. Just say:
"No, no, not this again," and abide the sorrow
for both Celtic Tiger cub, Ceasefire baby:
freed of blood, silence, the tears of tomorrow.

As Leaves Or Thieves

They're lying low in the back garden
light as leaves or thieves;
you're spooked and stock-still
and six years old again.
Eyes stare you down
from the untrimmed box hedge
without blinking, vanish
like asterisms. Wink of tattoo
and war-paint, axe-heads
knapped from flint
could gently tap the outline
of your skull forever.
This is how it happens at night,
in half-sleep or barely any: switchblades
of grass flick open, a welded
fence curls its black ironwork
into rust-gilded hooks down
the garden path's snaking stepping stones,
feather-finned arrows nock
in the dark, leaves sizzle—and under
your feet, grass slurps dewily.
Out in the wastepatch beyond the estate
a stolen car burns like funeral pyre,
molting sparks skyward, and
the moon, ripe for ambush, lights up
your hairless veins, its lotus cool
Catching—kindness unspilled.
The mind peels back,
soars and splinters like rubble.
Is there life out here? Is there mercy?

Violet Gibson*

For Annemarie Ní Churreáin

The jammed Lebel 8mm, as a principal of reason;
history hinged on a mere second of dead-eye

and all around her, the crowd's fawning reverence,
a bundle of Roman sticks, the open-palmed salute—

Il Duce's skull, ripe for a bullet. The shot misses
by inches as he averts his head, leaving the Lord's work

unfinished and yet fully executed. She pulls the trigger
a final time, her target seeing her fully now, a shawled

vindicator aiming to send him off, glory hallelujah
of fire and lead; something like sacrifice, units of beauty,

measured in impetus: better to die for God, with a hymn
in her ears, than to smash car windows, draw a better bead,

seeds of a wild notion rooted in her skull. She wonders:
aren't we all fascists by instinct? It's worth asking.

Sure who among us wouldn't prefer the world to comply
with our way of thinking? The worst outcomes result

from the finest intentions, after all, hence why she left
the convent that morning, gun cradled in a black shawl,

hand stretched out like a message from the Lord, varicose veins
lining her hand and wingbeats unheard between earth and the

heavens. From his nose bursts bloody disdain, but no testament
in her name bar psychiatric reports, a bastard distance kept.

*Irishwoman who attempted to assassinate Benito Mussolini
in Rome's Piazza del Campidoglio on April 7th, 1926.

Spring in the Sablon

In Brussels, I was advised to drink the beer as if it were wine
with all the measured sloth of the urbane fanatic
as smoky cumuli tapered the steeple, the May light
of rutted cobblestone curling into the antique market.

From my guide book's duty-free page, sly insights
leapt like flames from coal, like captives free of the pit,
scattering pigeons, useful gems I easily forgot.

Hear me above the atonal jazz on Rue Joseph Stevens,
the feral trio of bass, piano and sax roasting
an after-hours basement in many degrees of separation;
hear me in the Senne's ebb and the damp of plazas
drying in the fitful sunlight that peels back the mist,
in the benevolent maze of alleys and one-way avenues.

Look at the Palais de Justice, bristling with scaffolds.
That is where I would meet you, were you here, the chill
dissolving at your grin and kiss, in your hand I hold.

Monkey Gone to Heaven

Naturally, under the brownstones' squat shade,
    you see moss and weeds sprout up
from each thin, aged slit along an anterior patio,
    dusk's amber fume tingeing tar-black
fire escapes, neon spat through the windshield,
    the sun's molten crest left to ripple, stoke
behind Fenway Park, or the Charles unspooling
    ten million pounds of sludge into the ocean
like scrubbed silver. But to see beyond these,
    you remind yourself that it takes just a look
or word freighted with design, for love to begin
    or end. Being stuck in 5:00 p.m. traffic on
93 North is half the experience, in your dad's silver
    Honda-Accord, amid dump trucks and 4x4s,
beyond the reach of subway tunnels, with me
    riding shotgun, my palm on your knee, the stereo
tuned to "92.5 The River, Boston's independent
    radio" as Nirvana's 'Come as You Are' (the MTV
Unplugged version), replete with audience whoops
    and an extra rogue note slipped into the main
riff, starts up. We both say nothing, our voices
    bottled, stilled to a cool finish, and enjoy
the drive ahead. But there are things I should say
    that I'd rather you didn't hear just yet: the ex
I kissed and re-kissed without your knowledge,
    the girls I conjure up when I masturbate, the looks,
words and fucks held in inimical reserve—all of this
    I need to tell you now and only now,
on the road ahead, swept clear by headlights,
    while we still have the luxury of time.
                    (Massachusetts, 2017)

Lion's Den

I dam the deluge of headlines (climate change, Brexodus,
Syria, mortar bombs dumped in the North Channel,
Nursing strikes, writing scratched on the wall,
Consecrated graffiti, prophecies too dire for prose)
And in the hallway, stomach hollowed out to a pit,
Switch the heaters off (though we pay a flat rate),

Delete emails, sift through the buildup of rejections
That snowballed over the weekend, scour Jobs.ie,
Recall I've only two weeks left to go 'til my last payday.
Hours slash down to zero at the Dept. of Social Protection,
Ends seem met and then quickly unravel, savings drip
And every small sin necessary to survive piles up.

Lions are waking at my feet, a low-rumbled growl
Stirring from gullets as they forget their pelts
And sweep their tails from side to side. They prowl
Toward me, shaking fur from their manes' moult,
Eyes dilating and narrow, the flexed claw
And canines gritted behind their tightly-poised jaw—

This is what it's come to. Whatever point or purpose
I once had is melted in ether. With this profusion of time,
I find ways to occupy myself and ignore how close
To the brink I sit. I'm well past knowing shame
For saying, the job is the life raft I clung to, that I let rob
All that fury, collar it to a routine, 'cause having a job

Is bad enough, but having none is far worse.
All that wasted time before a tablet screen,
I dust off my CV, recite glib interview lines, force
Myself into industry-standard levels of keen,
Fix my game-face grin 'til it's positively glowing;
But really, I'm drained of all I need to keep going

I'm back walking on air as if on water, while
The last Linden Village sours in the fridge.

There's no room left for error, courage
Or even improvisation on my LinkedIn profile
And though the lions seem to sleep where they lie,
Once I turn to leave, they'll pounce on the sly.

Border Crossing

When checkpoints are reinstalled from Newry
to the Foyle, each soldier huddling with his gun
and camera, razor-wire taut to overextension,

inspections held in low-voiced urgency,
familiar whiff of smoke from a mirrored fire
it took decades to douse re-occupies the eye

and plucks out tears, what'll become of the side-road,
heavy with patrol's familiar rhythm, thorn-thickets
scorched deep by IEDs, craters from an asteroid?

I once believed that blood could be rinsed off,
scars soothed by talk of peace—but peace
is fragile here. Fragile as the notion of itself.

Headlines re-ask the national question, cease,
desist, leave it open, unanswered. Will bomb-proof
idols be re-set in stone, shootings set to increase,

blood purified of water, streetlights punched out,
skips brim over with the dregs of rubble?
All things un-considered, in the name of doubt:

Which neighbor will I see, if the border's visible?
Who can claim what right-of-way? Do I cross it
freely, into Derry or Tyrone? Or will old fevers boil

the marrowbone, long-running sore left unheard
like tonight's forecast or the lonely, choked
tick of a clock, being forced backward?

Hush

And if we lived in the States, I'd use
a police scanner to help myself sleep.
The crackly feed of car-jackings,
drive-bys and robberies long in progress
would rasp over the airwave
from a L.A.P.D. radio
straight into my earphones here,
in a New Hampshire guestroom.

Endowed with a flair for saving myself,
I carry exculpation,
dreaming the holy white blooms
of gunfire are aimed at me,
lumps of soft-nosed iron
poised to puncture my flesh,
ceding to sleep only when I know
the perps aren't headed our way.

Instead, we share a bed
that confers no sleep, and dusts
our dreams with older dread,
a blue-black moon blanching your eye
as you clench my hand to yours
while I sigh darkly, chew on alarms
nestling in the tangled brain.

I get up at 12:07, careful not to let
cold seep under the sheets,
try sleeping on the couch, wrapped
in a heavy blanket, the image
of your eyes' almond glint
keeping me calm 'til daybreak
when you leave the room,
and pull me back in under
the covers for hush, for lazier love.

Beltane Fire Festival in Edinburgh

Midnight, the cusp of spring, swirls coolly in
from nowhere; heralded by the timed shriek

of banshees, cold shower-spray, gyration
of flame, bonfires and tapers are lit as

a single decoy, scalding stars of April.
Dancers and drummers foment the fever,

their bare nipples hardened by the chill,
their limbs splashed in coloured spurts.

We melt each winter dreg on Carlton Hill
to the torchbearers' slow march, gulp our

cans of Stella; cinders of the goddess
crackle and perish amidst the columns

like bibelots, and the king's horned carcass
is an autopsy reborn, girlish and solemn.

Spellbound by paraffin, ablaze as the city,
we have hours yet before we'll see dawn.

But when the smoke clears, the columns are sooty
with fused, tar-like blots, waxed in the early sun.

Outage

When the power cut out,
the only light left in our flat was the whirring glow
off my laptop, milky and stark as the risen moonlight.
Impermanent as ice,
the sudden silence did little to calm us.

Corralled in sleeping bags,
we detached from each other with the slowness
of glaciers adrift in meltwater,
and I wished I could join you again in sleep

where the grip of commitment was loosened
and we could inhale the old savory heat.

*

We have outgrown love
just as we outgrew the grass on that brittle riverbank.

The silence does little to calm us. It's been long underway,
we realize as we shiver and stalactites hang
like verdicts in the hallway; it leaves us frozen
as if among headlights, floods our ears,

mists and unmoors our eyes, makes waves
of pale flecks rise slowly to our skulls. A rumble

of ice calving sets in; the door of what used
to be our room is double-locked
as cold fronts swirl in from all longitudes.

The bulbs sizzle and flicker again. I get my suitcase
ready, unsure to hurry or to drag my heels.
You walk out into the crisp sunrise, while
I gather up flotsam of the last three years.

After the Bailey

i.m. Gerry Conlon, 1954-2014

After the Bailey, he walked the streets
at sundown, inhaling death like a coal fume,
his face bristly, boots scuffed to shreds,
clutching a life he knew he'd never resume.

Dawn smiled sadly on the Falls Road.
He heard a drunk's red-raw laughter,
worn out from dancing to the music
of the spheres, the calm of hereafter,

the sprawl of a city in guarded remission.
For all things, he felt he stood accused.
He had to remind himself that, in prison,
the sun and moon are easily confused.

The past is another country, they say.
One he would never emigrate from.
The last sound he needed to hear
was the fateful echo of his own name,

chanted by protesters, spat by prison guards,
or declared, at the pleasure of a judge,
as one more public enemy: an iron verdict,
overseen from the altitudes of privilege.

He pushed invisible rocks from street
to street, stooping against a bulk
only he could feel, his nerve centre
scorched by trauma's molten milk.

Another day to endure, Gerry Conlon.
The sun rises for your trampled benefit,
warming the blameless in a world where
fortune favors only the well-connected.

Provence, 2016

I.

The road is tasseled with vineyards and vine-stalks green
as springtime, sweat of olive and pear
soak my t-shirt through, and starlings fly in flocks.
The famed friction between mistral and midsummer
has yet to arrive, but blood irrigates the soil
of this tourist's Eden. A slow-burning haze
warps the far-off Luberon, and the lofty windmill,
with blades long as the old law or sunrays,
built to grind out cereal or barley, stands
like a milestone on the hot ridge. My twenty-fourth
summer. I might grow to love this sultry province,
birthplace of troubadours, its cypresses staring north
like a Van Gogh nocturne, the mimosa's natal wince
at my touch, the bulk of fate forcing my hands.

II.

Such barefaced sentimentality has little place
in the world, yet even the small farmhands here
show a care to the groves that cash won't replace.
Earth-scarring winds whisper to the lavender,
and the bullfrogs' snarl is chronic as clockwork.
It is late June: the beer tastes frothy and calm,
the last peach harvest is over, gates with electric bolts
lie open, palls of dust rise like the fine atom
of a genie, and the ruby hover of a dragonfly
specifies the hour when the upstairs window shutters
slam their displeasure at my tenancy
of the villa in rippled wind, jolting me unawares.
I am a failure who has had his taste of triumph
in that sun-drunk sky, this aged pasture of wheat,
the swimming pool's shimmer, a late-blooming nymph
unripe for flight, in boneless recoil from the heat.

Cais de Colunas

The AirBnB listing read like a manifesto;
ours was seventh plane on the runaway.
Quarter of an hour 'til we were airborne
for Lisbon, jet-lagged at the terminal,
we ignored the engines' whirring grind
to life, the pilot's apology for the delay.

Amid trams and colonial caskets, engraved caravels
on a monastery wall, suffused by *fado*, held me.
Eroded by surf and birdshit, two marble-headed
columns sank gently into the estuary where *poentes*
gently collided and marble steps led to the silt,
carved with a prayer-blessing for sailors;
we couldn't make it out, nor even cared to.

Factor 50 bubbled on our cheeks, sea-air retched
on a compass rose as we plastered on smiles
for the camera, clasped fingers; we looked good together,
glamorous, nearly. But you'd each and every
right to hate me, even with sunsparkles winking

on the Tagus' azure swell below the gantries.
Look back on this with some fondness, if you're able;
look back with some care, on me as you
thought I was, if you can, look back on the ash
swept and quenched by the dusky tide,
and look back on love, as we knew it once.

Two Visionaries

1.   Artemisia Gentileschi

Your hands were soiled from a lifetime of paint
And, as the bronze-splashed palette dried to morsels
Of chroma, aficionados took up the cum-slick hunt
For a neatly-engraved icon, malefactors in their cells.

What you truly loved was the bone-white canvas
And your father's Hellenic instruction to execute
Each finer detail in deep red charm, the smudgy kiss
Of brushwork moistening trauma to a girdle of light.

Colour schemes throb in the still of your studio,
Hover solid as the shade that tongues the landscape.
By your unflagging craft, precise and poised to

Sweep away the embers of gutted apprenticeship
To a clichéd school and its dusty style, your pilgrimage:
Allegories of art, of life, rendered in your own image.

2. Rephrasing
   After Sean Ruane's 'Rushes'

(On Mickey Rourke in "The Wrestler")

It's been said that when he first read the script,
Mickey hated it, along with what he saw
As the fake, stage-managed meat market
Of pro-wrestling itself. So he rephrased nearly all
His dialogue, line by line, using moments
From his own crippled life, up to and including
The piteous speech he lays down from the ring
In the climax at Asbury Park Convention Hall.

A raw failed brother, cauliflower-eared,
Still hungry to bleed for his art; I didn't believe
In the stony cocoon he sheathed himself in—

Only in the blunt eloquence—the torn
Heart he held up to the light, steroid artistry
Left in embers. And so the act goes.

Pebbles

Later on, a search party of sanderlings
Hustle at low tide among the sand flats
In ivory-winged agitation, haggling

Over fish carcass, blubber fillet, barnacle eye
And seizing up all entrails before rats
Try to stake their own claim under the sky.

They have no leader, nor need one. Instinct
Is their fuel, inborn range and velocity
Prevailing where sand and surf are linked.

Pebbles of intent bulge in my pocket
When I see a yellowed thrush-skull pressed
Deep in the sand, each eye socket

The shape of bullet-holes and bloody feathers
Scattered like frills where a dying wave crests
As I move to sink in any and all weathers.

(Boston, 2017)

The Blind Leading the Legless

You walk slowly, a parody of deliberation,
down the ward's muggy corridor, past
the nurse's station and endless bleep
of monitors, head bowed and shoulders
hunched like the villain in a silent film,
unable to sit still or stay in motion for too
long as the pain rocketed up your spine.
Just like the blind leading the legless:
blackened blood-crust, whitecap of tablets
fizzing in a glass of water, irregularly sipped,
wires draining you alive, the pure siesta
of painkillers wiped clean of dreams.
Your arms are folded as you sit slumped,
half-asleep with the telly still going.
Your gritted teeth and growled breath
when you stand up and go for a piss
or a final smoke outside, lighting a new one
off the old before visiting hours finish.

Called back in for an MRI, the view
from your window a patchwork
of slate roofs, frost-sugared footpaths,
cranes, desultory traffic plainsong.
I rarely came to visit, or even texted
or phoned, except on your last day.
You were out of cigarette papers, I recall;
I handed you some Rizlas from the Spar
round the corner. On your locker,
your Halfzware lay unsmoked. Nearly
fifteen months of visits, overnight stays,
in a Palexia haze and expertly-starched
bedclothes, nurses coming and going,
sent you off to yet another prescribed
slumber; you played the waiting game
in shifts of sleep, refill, repeat.

And on the day of your operation,
the red-crusted suture tracking
down your spine, your blood thinned
to cheap wine. The morning you
were discharged, the first blood moon
in fourteen years swam in the sky. You
walked painlessly again, though still slow,
your nerves under fire from the elements.
A set of piano keys grinned warmly
when you arrived back at the house.

Warmth

For Julie O' Brien

You have a way of going quiet and nodding
at the space between things, in the rare times
when I visit you at the house you raised us in,
or on long walks taken through grassland.
There are mornings when you'd be glad to die,
and others when you holler your thanks to heaven
for being able to witness yet another sunrise.
And yet also, there's your natural flair of affection,
the mirror-like orbit of your concern for us,
that I, too often, am powerless to return. I hear
your voice on the phone, keeping me informed
of choir and cancer, holidays to Lisbon and the cat,
'til my lunch break reaches an end and we must
let each other go again. You have a way of laughing out
loud to fill each room to capacity, and the rest
of us can't help but join in. Last week, when the snow
was at its heaviest, I tried piling logs in our fireplace,
crumpled newsprint and lighters for kindling,
hoping to send some warmth out to you,
wherever you happened to be. Knowing you're
here is better than anything lost or gained.

Blues for Louis

Upstairs in JJ's, no-one else could command
the stately darkness—sitting cross-legged centre
stage, spectacled eyes shut, working his way

through a solo, the Gibson relaxedly cradled for riff
and melody to waft among the punters, his amp
squatting in smooth licks and swings. A noble nerve

plucked by the bassline, cymbal hisses slithered
downstage as crumpled sheet music fell off its stand,
pianokeys wove a deep web of medley around him:

rare tones abide with "Moonlight Serenade", "Billies
Bounce", "All The Things You Are" in wiry tension,
and the relief that can follow. Pints were sipped

in-between tunes, fivers, tenners and coins reluctantly
thumbed as a final round was bought, the barman's holler
for last orders echoed up from the keg room, sudsy

glasses left on the bar where I'd lean in forlorn hope
of getting served, still drawn in by his rhythm: it was shelter
and purgatory at once. And just outside the sweat-glazed

wall and sloped doorway: a crushed rollie winked up
from damp tarmac, a chip bag's oily lure; as I waited
blearily on a Nitelink for rescue, the bus stop

shimmered. Only men who work miracles are bored
by them—but I knew, even then, that I was after
hearing his miracle, the stately darkness at hand.

Acknowledgments

"Medal," and "Breadline Gladiators," *The Hennessey New Irish Writing Page*; "Mountpleasant Aubade," *Banshee Press*; "Lion's Den," "Violet Gibson", and "As Leaves or Thieves," *The Agonist Journal*; "Outage", *The Blue Mountain Review*; "In the Ivy Exchange", *The Scum Gentry Alternative Arts and Media Network*; "Rope Jockey and "Rooftop Blues," *Cassandra Voices*; "Artemisa Gentilsechi," and "Beltane Fire Festival in Edinburgh," *The Galway Review*; "Monkey Gone to Heaven", *Fresh Air Poetry*, "A Volunteer" *Zymbol*; "Prey," *Deep Water Literary Journal*; "After the Bailey", "Here, Paddy"; "Rephrasing," *The Lonely Crowd Anthology*; "Immram," *The Sea Anthology*; "Devil Eire I" and "Spring in the Sablon," *Flare*; "Rapids", *Ink, Sweat And Tears*.

"John de Courcy Ireland" was both displayed as part of the 'Pale Project Exhibition', devised by LexIcon writer-in-residence Selina Guinness in 2016.

Several poems from the 'Sea Batteries' sequence were written for CoastMonkey. ie, the maritime website specializing in natural and historical exploration of the Irish coast. "Achaemenides", "The Liner Reina del Pacifico during Sea Trials", and "Bádóirí" were among the poems featured on the site. The title poem was featured in the *People on the Pier* anthology, edited by Marian Keyes and Betty Stenson, published by New Island Books, September 2018

"Border Crossing" was featured in the April 2019 edition of *ROPES Literary Journal*, published annually by MA students of Literature & Publishing at NUI Galway.

"Sea State Martello" was filmed as a spoken-word piece by Dublin filmmaker Alan Dunne of Stubborn Monkey Productions, and released in June 2019 as part of that year's Bloomsday celebrations.

"Maude Jane Delap" won the Write by the Sea Kilmore Quay Poetry Competition 2019.

Daniel Wade is a poet and playwright from Dublin, Ireland. In January 2017, his play *The Collector* opened the 20th anniversary season of the New Theatre, Dublin. His spoken-word album *Embers and Earth*, available for download on iTunes and Spotify, launched the previous October at the National Concert Hall. A prolific performer, Daniel has featured at many festivals including Electric Picnic, Body and Soul, and the 2019 International Literature Festival (ILFD). In January 2020 his radio drama *Crossing the Red Line* was broadcast on RTE Radio 1 Extra, and later won a silver award at the New York Festivals Radio Awards for Best Digital Drama. He is also the author of the e-chapbook *Iceberg Relief*, published by Underground Voices in 2017. Daniel was the Hennessy New Irish Writing winner for April 2015 in The Irish Times, and his poetry and short fiction have appeared in over two dozen publications since 2012.

Website http://danielwadeauthor.com/
Facebook https://www.facebook.com/DanielWadeau...
Instagram: https://www.picbon.com/user/dan_wade_...
Soundcloud https://soundcloud.com/daniel-wade-7
Youtube https://www.youtube.com/channel/UCk2n...
Spotify https://open.spotify.com/album/1c9AbP...
Apple Music https://itunes.apple.com/us/album/emb...

Previous Publications: "Medal," and "Breadline Gladiators," *The Hennessey New Irish Writing Page*; "Mountpleasant Aubade," *Banshee Press*; "Lion's Den," "Violet Gibson", and "As Leaves or Thieves," *The Agonist Journal*; "Outage", *The Blue Mountain Review*; "Red Cow Nocturne", *Dodging The Rain*; "Border Crossing", *ROPES Literary Journal*; "In the Ivy Exchange", *The Scum Gentry Alternative Arts and Media Network*; "Rope Jockey and "Rooftop Blues," *Cassandra Voices*; "Artemisa Gentilsechi," and "Beltane Fire Festival in Edinburgh," *The Galway Review*; "Monkey Gone to Heaven", *Fresh Air Poetry*, "A Volunteer" *Zymbol*; "Prey," *Deep Water Literary Journal*; "After the Bailey", "Here, Paddy"; "Rephrasing," *The Lonely Crowd Anthology*; "Immram," *The Sea Anthology*; "Devil Eire I" and "Spring in the Sablon," *Flare*; "Rapids", *Ink, Sweat And Tears*. "John de Courcy Ireland" was both displayed as part of the 'Pale Project Exhibition', devised by LexIcon writer-in-residence Selina Guinness in 2016. Several poems from the 'Sea Batteries' sequence were written for CoastMonkey.ie, the maritime website specializing in natural and historical exploration of the Irish coast. "Achaemenides", "The Liner Reina del Pacifico during Sea Trials", and "Bádóirí" were among the poems featured on the site. The title poem was featured in the People on the Pier anthology, edited by

Marian Keyes and Betty Stenson, published by New Island Books, September 2018."Border Crossing" was featured in the April 2019 edition of ROPES Literary Journal, published annually by MA students of Literature & Publishing at NUI Galway. "Sea State Martello" was filmed as a spoken-word piece by Dublin filmmaker Alan Dunne of Stubborn Monkey Productions, and released in June 2019 as part of that year's Bloomsday celebrations. "Maude Jane Delap" won the Write by the Sea Kilmore Quay Poetry Competition 2019.

www.ingramcontent.com/pod-product-compliance
Lightning Source LLC
Chambersburg PA
CBHW021150090426
42740CB00008B/1032